Elizabeth,
Enjoy the book with my warmest regards.

[signature]

Sacramento

CALIFORNIA

A PHOTOGRAPHIC PORTRAIT

Photography by Steve Pate-Newberry

Narrative by Michelle Alberigi McKenzie

TWIN LIGHTS PUBLISHERS | ROCKPORT, MASSACHUSETTS

First published in the
United States of America by:

Twin Lights Publishers, Inc.
Rockport, Massachusetts 01966
Telephone: (978) 546-7398
www.twinlightspub.com

ISBN: 978-1-934907-62-7

10 9 8 7 6 5 4 3 2 1

(opposite)
Sacramento Skyline

(frontispiece)
Pony Express Monument

(jacket front)
Tower Bridge

(jacket back)
River Walk and Old Sacramento

Book design by:
SYP Design & Production, Inc.
www.sypdesign.com

Printed in China

W elcome to Sacramento, the capital of California—the 5th largest economy in the world. Sacramento is the bustling center of the forward motion that California takes onto the world stage, be it as an environmental leader, taking the farm to fork movement to new heights, or as a leader in the fight for human rights.

Sacramento has been the center of human activity in California for hundreds of years because of the rich resources of the Sacramento River and the Sacramento Valley. California's first incorporated city in 1849, Sacramento's history is filled with the golden dreams of the 1848 Gold Rush, the Pony Express, the railroad, education, and prosperity.

Education is important to Sacramentans and California State University, Sacramento, enrolls over 28,000 students a year, offering 151 Bachelor's degrees, 69 Master's degrees, 28 teaching credentials, and 2 Doctoral degrees.

The city is known by many names: "The City of Trees," "The Farm to Fork Capital," "The Camellia Capital of the World," "The Big Tomato," and to the locals, it's just "Sac," or "Sactown." Call it what you like, Sacramentans are proud of their city—where it's been and where it's going.

It's here that floods and the California Gold Rush and entrepreneurs changed the city. And it's here that the Pony Express made its 1,966 mile runs between St. Joseph, MO, and Sacramento in 10 days or less, until the opening of the transcontinental telegraph in October 1861 made it obsolete.

It's here that the "Big Four," Leland Stanford, Collis Huntington, Mark Hopkins, and Charles Crocker, met and built the Central Pacific Railroad that made it possible to travel from west to east across the country by way of the Transcontinental Railroad.

Photographer Steve Pate-Newberry focuses his love and his camera on his hometown with spectacular results. See the city through Steve's lens in these pages and you will gain a new appreciation for this important city.

Tower Bridge (*opposite*)

Replacing the old drawbridge in 1935, the Tower Bridge, also known as the Sacramento River Bridge, epitomizes Streamline Moderne—a late art deco style of architecture. The road from the bridge leads spectacularly to the Capitol Building and the 40-acre Capitol Park.

State Capitol *(above and left)*

The State Capitol, built in 1860–1874, is enshrined in Capitol Park, a glorious 40 acres of plants from around the world with over 800 trees and flowering shrubs. The park's purpose was to showcase the Capitol building, and it once housed the 1884 Agricultural Pavilion for the State Fair exhibits.

California State Capitol

Efforts were made to relocate the Capitol even after it became the permanent seat. San Jose, Oakland, Berkeley, and Monterey each tried to win the distinc-tion due to the glitter of the increased commerce and prestige that it would bring. Sacramento got the prize.

Sisters of Mercy Statue *(top)*

Five members of the religious institute Sisters of Mercy arrived in San Francisco in 1857, finding their way to Sacramento to minister to Gold Rush miners, homeless, abandoned children, and the sick. The statue was erected on their property, where the Capitol now stands. In 1860, the state bought the property.

Pathway Along State Capitol *(bottom)*

Surrounding the Capitol Building, Capitol Park is always accessible. Enjoyed by locals as well as visitors, the grounds are a place to walk, meet friends, and to enjoy events. The 10 blocks are anchored between 10th and 16th and L and N streets.

California State Capitol

Although other cities vied to be the state capitol, Sacramento became the permanent seat in 1860. The Capitol Building's Roman architecture was designed as a smaller version of the Nation's Capitol Building in Washington, DC. The Capitol hosts the California State Legislature and the governor's office.

Governor's Mansion *(above and opposite)*

Built in 1877 and known as the Executive Mansion, this was home to thirteen governors and their families from 1903 to 1967. After that time, it remained without a governor until 2015 when it was renovated. Today, it once again is the official residence for the governor.

California State Library (top)

Established in 1850 to keep the state's facts and documents in a central location, the library collects and preserves history and is the central reference and research library for the state government and legislature. Additionally, it aids California's public libraries by directing state and federal funds for their support.

Sacramento City Hall (bottom)

This 1911 Beaux Arts–style building, designed by Rudolph A. Herold, was recently restored and while it retains its original splendor, its temporary annex was removed. It now sports a curving, two-story arcade and includes energy efficient systems throughout. The outdoor area offers a place to rest for visitors.

Sacramento River

The Sacramento River, once Rio de los Sacramentos, is the largest in California. Farming and ranching replaced its once abundant fisheries and, while used by outdoor enthusiasts for recreation, the river provides water to over half of the state's population and irrigates much of Central and Southern California.

Delta King Riverboat

Docked along the riverfront in Old Sacramento, this 285-foot-long riverboat is a floating hotel, restaurant, and theater. Overnight guests enjoy an opulent lobby, views of the river, and an award-winning restaurant, The Delta Bar and Grill. The Delta King is just minutes from many of Old Sacramento's shops and attractions.

Delta King Riverboat *(top and bottom)*

Christened in 1927, the *Delta King* made daily, 10.5-hour voyages between San Francisco and Sacramento. The Golden Gate and Bay bridges were completed in 1937 and 1938 and put an end to this era. Today, the *Delta King* is permanently moored on the Sacramento River.

River Walk Park (above and opposite)

The River Walk Park stretches from the Tower Bridge to one block south of the I Street Bridge. *A Life's Ride* by artist Terrence Martin is one of a few installations along the walkway. Educational signs about the settlement of Sacramento and the river's natural habitat are set along the trail.

Zaggurat (right)

Built in 1997, the Ziggurat office building is ten stories high, built in a pyramid style, and houses the California Department of General Services. Designed by architect Edwin Kado to favor the ancient Mesopotamian ziggurats, it sits on more than 7 acres adjacent to the Tower Bridge.

River Walk Park *(top and bottom)*

Relax along the banks or walk your dog in this 7.5-acre park that sits opposite Old Sacramento and located near the Ziggurat. Here you can also enjoy the city's summer concert series and the Riverbank Music Festival. This park offers walking paths, picnic tables, and more, all with wheelchair accessibility.

River Walk Park *(opposite)*

Located near West Sacramento, this 9.5-mile, round-trip trail is wonderful for taking in the natural beauty you'll find all along the river. Nearby is Raley's Landing and a dock that provides access for fishing enthusiasts. The area is also accessible by water taxi.

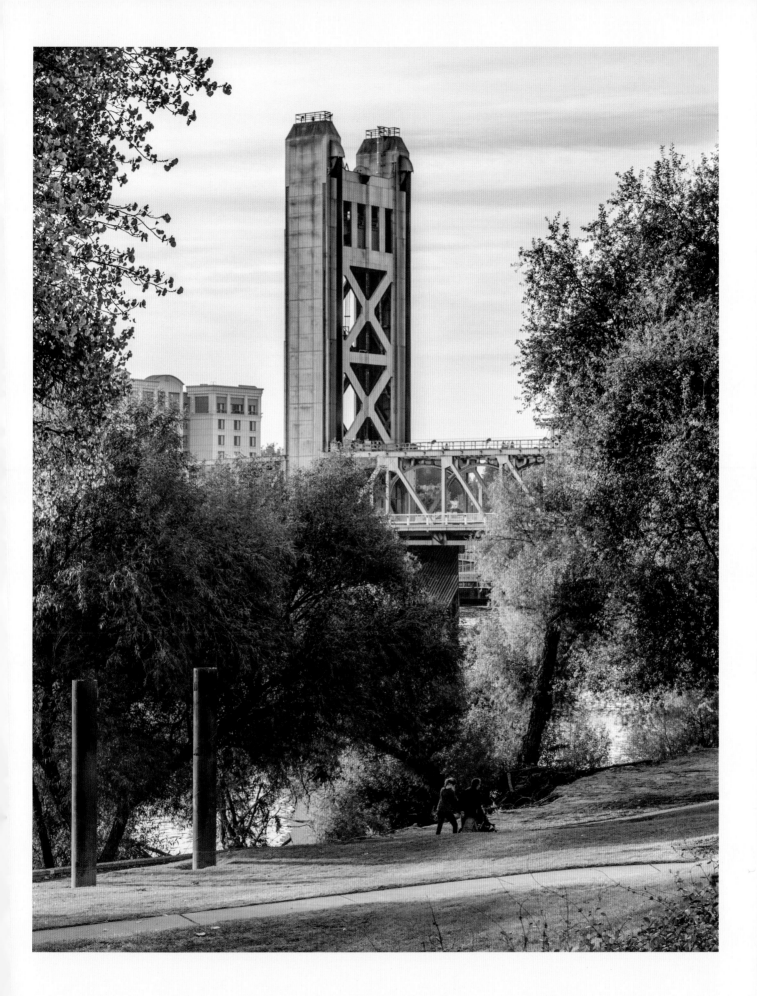

Evening Lights *(above and left)*

The Sacramento skyline is accented by the glow from the Tower Bridge, both day and night. Changes to the skyline are always taken into consideration as city developers look to add office space and housing. The gateway to the Capitol, Tower Bridge is undeniably the city's most iconic landmark.

Tower Bridge

Hailed for its architectural design and streamlined appearance, Tower Bridge is considered one of the most beautiful vertical lift bridges in operation. In 1976, the bridge's silver paint was replaced with a yellow-ochre color, which casts a warm glow when illuminated in the evening light.

Water Treatment Plant Intake Pier and Access Bridge *(above and left)*

Located just north of the new Sacramento River Water Inlet building, the old water treatment Plant Intake Pier sits along the river. When it was first constructed between 1921–1923 it was the most modern facility in the west and utilized a sand filtration technique.

Tower Bridge *(top)*

Originally a swinging steel drawbridge, the Tower Bridge was replaced in 1935 by the current structure with its vertical lift that allows the passage of large boats and ships with tall masts. Here, the bridge has opened for the sailing ship *Hawaiian Chieftain* to pass through.

Sacramento River Skyline *(bottom)*

The Sacramento River played a crucial role in the development of the city and the Sacramento Valley, providing access for trade and travel. Today, the river and its banks are home to a multitude of species of birds, fish, crustaceans and riparian plants, while offering a scenic respite for visitors.

Sacramento River Water Intake
Structure *(top, bottom, and opposite)*

Situated on the Sacramento River, the
water intake facility offers grand views of
the city while also protecting fish through
its fish-screen project. Attractive as well
as interesting, this new Sacramento River
landmark is topped with a large silver
feather by sculptor Phill Evans.

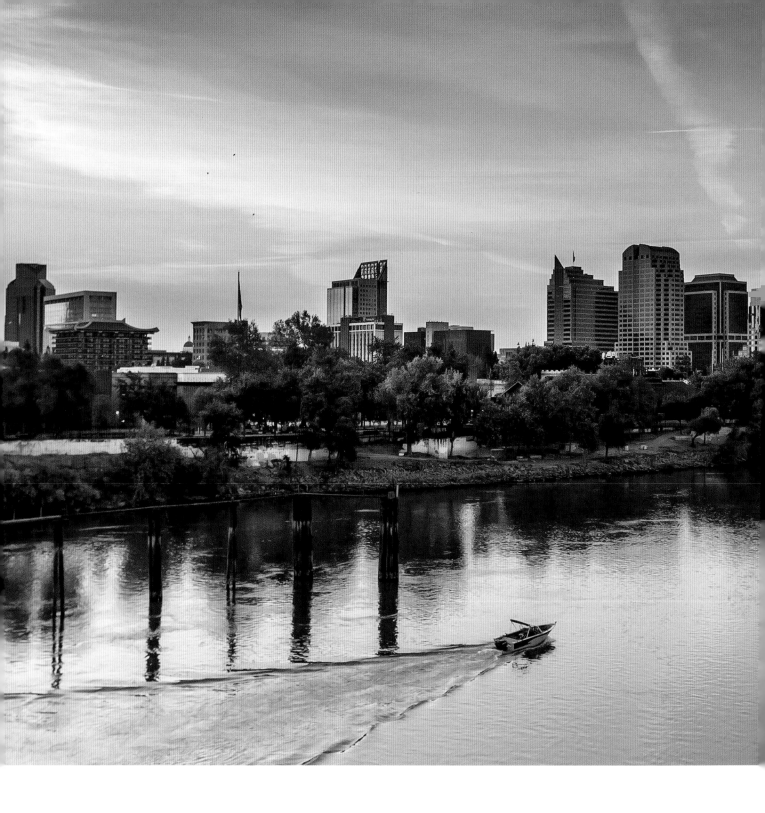

Sacramento River Skyline

The gentle wake of a lone boat stirs the river's reflections at dusk. In the background are the *Delta King* and the Tower Bridge. Some of the city's tallest buildings that comprise its skyline include the Wells Fargo Center, U.S. Bank Tower, and Park Tower.

Hawaiian Chieftain

An annual visitor to the Sacramento River, this 103-foot contemporary ketch arrives in November and offers educational tours for the public. Built of steel in 1988 by Lahaina Welding Co., Ltd, the design was influenced by early colonial passenger and coastal packets that traded among Atlantic coastal towns.

Tower Bridge (top)

In any light, the golden glow of the Tower Bridge can be seen across much of the Sacramento River. Painted yellow, the bridge's color matches the gold-leafed cupola of the State Capitol. Public boat docks offer dockage for boaters and are conveniently located on the Old Sacramento waterfront.

Sacramento River and Old Town (bottom)

The *Delta King* is docked off of Old Town on the Sacramento River—the first commercial area for the new town of Sacramento. By the mid-1800s the river was bustling with steamboats transporting crops to San Francisco, which helped transform the trading colony and stockade into the major city it is today.

Old Sacramento Historic Park (top)

Attracting over 5 million visitors annually, the park's 28 acres offer the original historic waterfront beginnings of Sacramento. Most of the buildings have survived through renovation and care and date from the 19th century. Their architecture, while attributed to Victorian gold miners, also exhibit Spanish influence.

Big Four Building (bottom)

Declared a California Historical Landmark in 1961, the Big Four Building was originally three buildings. Named after its original owners, Leland Stanford, Mark Hopkins, Charles Crocker and Collis Huntington, who were called the Big Four for their joint effort to link the First Transcontinental Railway from California to the East.

Booth Building

The Booth Building was the home and wholesale grocery business of Newton Booth, who later became a California Senator in 1862–63, a California governor 1871–75, and a U.S. Senator 1875–81. From the roof platform, cargo ships were signaled as they approached Sacramento to secure purchases ahead of their competitors.

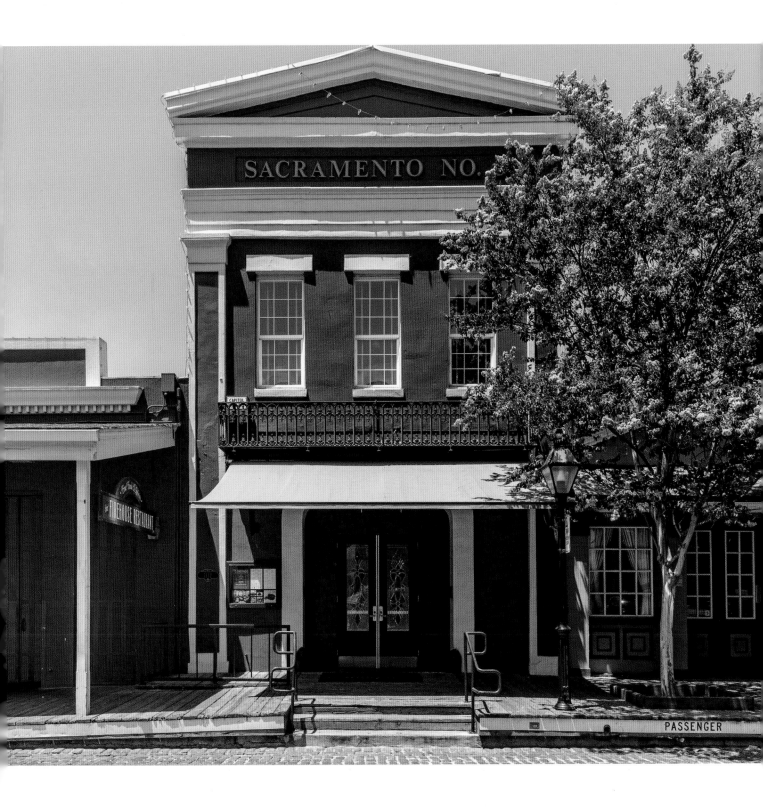

Old Sacramento *(opposite top and bottom)*

A graceful arch welcomes visitors to Old Sacramento. Carriage rides provide a different perspective on the 28-acre historic park including museums, restaurants, shops, and the *Delta King* paddleboat hotel. Some carriages offer rides around the State Capitol Building and Capitol Park.

Sacramento No. 3 *(above)*

Built in 1853, Sacramento Engine Company No. 3 was built to house California's first fire department. In 1872 it became the state's first paid fire department. Painstakingly renovated to preserve the building, the old firehouse has served as The Firehouse Restaurant since 1960, a premier destination for fine dining.

Mounted Police *(opposite top)*

The Sacramento Police Department has operated a mounted police unit since 1998, providing a high-profile law-enforcement presence in the parks as well as at special events and dignitary visits. They can be spotted riding through various parks in Sacramento and Old Sacramento, often stopping to talk to visitors.

Old Sacramento *(opposite bottom)*

The streets of Old Sacramento retain their Victorian Old West look. The B.F. Hastings & Co. Building was the western terminus of the Pony Express during most of its short existence. The building now houses the old Supreme Court and Wells Fargo History Museum.

Old Schoolhouse Museum *(top and bottom)*

This replica of a one-room schoolhouse was typical in the Sacramento Valley during the late 1800s and early 1900s. It is filled with photos, books, desks and other antiques of the time, including a pot-belly stove. Celebrate a reunion or wedding or have a spelling bee at the Old Schoolhouse.

Pioneer Park (opposite top)

Originally the home of the local butcher shop, City Market, the building has changed many times over the years until it was finally demolished. Today, Pioneer Park sits at the original ground before the area was raised to protect against flooding. Displayed here are cast-iron columns from original dwellings.

Pioneer Telegraph Station (opposite bottom)

Erroneously called the Pony Express Terminal, the first transcontinental telegraph message was transmitted here to the State Telegraph Company on October 24, 1861, thus forcing the closure of the Pony Express two days later. Western Union Telegraph later operated from this site between 1868–1915.

Ebner's Hotel (above)

The stylish Ebner Hotel, built in 1856 by Charles and Francis Ebner, operated as a hotel for a century, but by the early 1930s the hotel and surrounding area fell into disrepair. Demolished in 2003, it was rebuilt in 2010 with the exterior resembling the original building and with modern interiors.

River City Saloon *(opposite top)*

Until 1871, the River City Saloon was one of Sacramento's first houses of ill repute before becoming Parker French's Saloon. Renovated in 2007 to its original grandeur, today the establishment is best known for its delicious deli sandwiches and Old West sarsaparilla.

Old Town Walk *(above and opposite bottom)*

Wooden planks enhance the feel of walking back into the 19th-century Old West. With plenty of unique boutiques, gift shops, restaurants, and candy stores, visitors are sure to find an interesting souvenir as they take a leisurely stroll through Sacramento's past.

Sacramento Visitors Center (top)

Newly remodeled and offering expanded accessibility, the Sacramento Visitors Center is the hub for learning about new exhibits with interactive elements in this unique historic park. The center is well equipped to help and inform their many visitors about Old Sacramento as well as other parts of the city.

Theatre of Lights (bottom)

Kicking off on Thanksgiving Eve, Macy's Theatre of Lights is a concept theater on the balconies of surrounding buildings, using lights and sounds. In particular is the production of 'Twas the Night Before Christmas. The production is set in 1857 Sacramento and is one of the area's favorite holiday events.

Wells Fargo History Museum (opposite)

Starting in California in 1852, Wells Fargo created a plan to provide express and banking services to California, which launched the Pony Express, a lone rider acting as courier, transporting bills, mail, money, and gold. Today, the museum offers exhibits highlighting stagecoach history, the telegraph, and gold discovery.

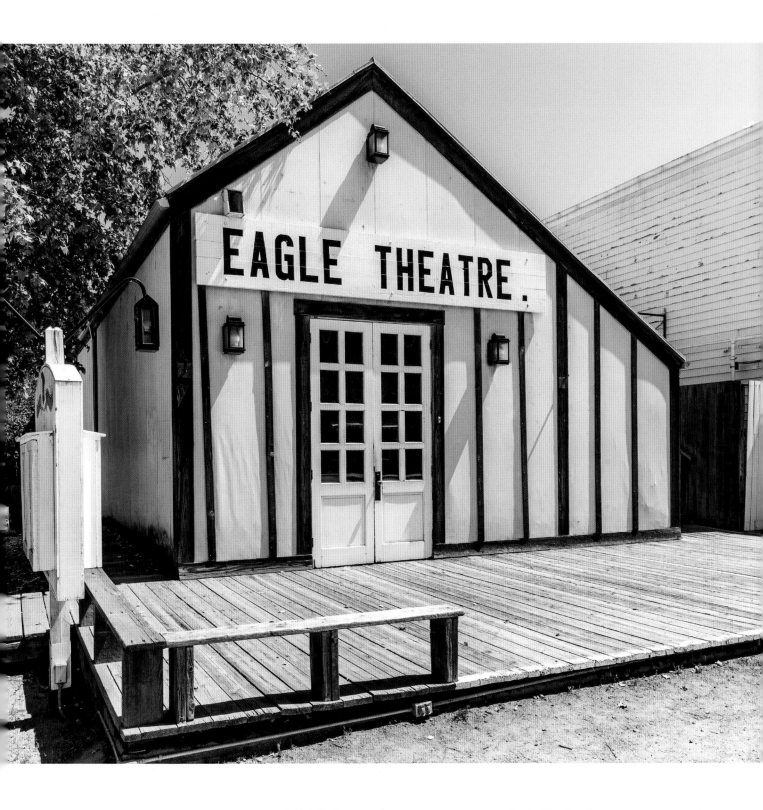

C.M & T. Co. *(opposite top)*

The Connecticut Mining and Trading Company, a simple building in the Gold Rush and Commerce area of Old Sacramento, was once home to several merchandise and auction businesses, Crowell, McDowell and Company, McDowell and Company and Crowell, Dudley and McDowell—all associated with Thomas McDowell.

Eagle Theatre *(above and opposite bottom)*

Constructed of wood and canvas in 1849, the Eagle Theatre was the first permanent theater in California. Here gold miners and pioneers were able to forget their problems. Destroyed by the flood in 1850, the building was reconstructed from the original theatre and today it offers programs to school groups in grades 4–6.

What Cheer House *(above)*

Built in 1853 and believed to be named after the common gold rush salutation, "what cheer, partner?" the hotel was raised an entire story in 1863 to protect it against future flooding. Renovated and modernized in the 1960s, today the What Cheer House is owned by Stage Nine Entertainment, Inc.

Old Sacramento Alley *(left)*

This view from Firehouse Alley, a partially cobblestoned street, looks up to the Ebner's Hotel. Recently rebuilt, its exterior closely resembles the distinct design of the original hotel, including ornate balconies and decorative windows that overlook K Street. Professional offices occupy its two upper floors.

Daily Union

The *Daily Union*, later called the *Sacramento Daily Union*, was a daily newspaper founded in 1851 and ran for the next 143 years, keeping a local focus on the concerns of Sacramento and the mining and agricultural communities. In 1858, it was the first California paper to print a double-sheet daily.

Adams & Company Building
(above and right)

Located in what was then Sacramento's business center, Adams and Company occupied this building from 1853 to 1855. The building also housed the Alta Telegraph Company, Wells Fargo & Co, California State Telegraph Company, Pacific Express Co, California State Co, and Sacramento City Bank.

Tehama Block and Central Pacific Railroad *(opposite top and bottom)*

The reconstructed Tehama Block building was home to several businesses including wholesale and retail stores, groceries, and stationary stores. Today, Skalet Family Jewelers occupies the space selling exquisite jewelry. The Central Pacific Passenger Station takes you back in time to 1876 where the J.W. Bowker steam locomotive is housed.

Old Town Train Depot (top)

The Central Pacific Railroad building was reconstructed to look exactly as it did in the 1860s. The freight depot was the major freight transport of daily arrivals and departures on the transcontinental railroad. The passenger station is just north of this building.

Old Town Waterfront (bottom)

Old Sacramento glows at night from the lights of commerce reflecting off the water. Take the trails along the waterfront to enjoy spectacular views of the city at night and to enjoy a colorful view of Old Sacramento and the railroad.

Old Town Historic Railway

Owned by the California Railroad Museum, the Sacramento Southern Railroad preserves the railway's history. Each weekend from April through September the museum presents 45-minute, roundtrip train rides where visitors can experience the sights, smells, and sounds of these historic locomotives.

Caboose and Steam Locomotive
(top and bottom)

On display outside the California State Railroad Museum is this brightly painted 1952 Union Pacific caboose (top). Steam locomotive Granite Rock No. 10 (bottom) was built for the US Army in 1942. Owned by the Sacramento Southern Railroad, it was put into tourism service in 1997.

Old Railroad Tours

Trains still run through Old Sacramento, moving both freight and passengers, but for a unique trip take an excursion through the California State Railroad Museum on the Sacramento Southern Railroad. These rides include closed coach cars, open-air gondolas, and a first-class observation car.

California State Railroad Museum
(above and right)

The California State Railroad Museum has over 225,000 square feet of exhibit space to showcase its collection of locomotives and cars. It also presents many engaging and interactive exhibits that explore the times surrounding trains and how they impacted life in Sacramento and the United States.

Historic Locomotives
(opposite top and bottom)

Twenty-one meticulously restored locomotives and cars offer a unique look into Sacramento's past, which include 19 steam locomotives from 1862 to 1944. Fewer than 45 full-size steam locomotives from before 1880 exist in the United States, and eight of them can be seen here at the museum.

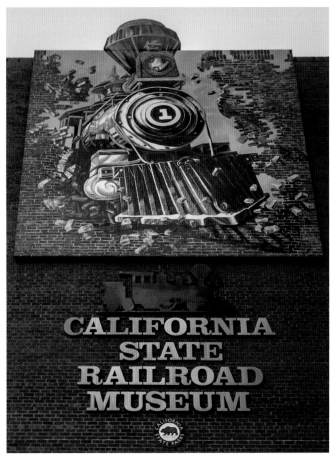

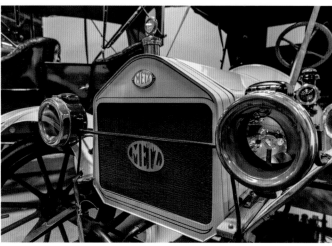

California Automobile Museum
(top and bottom)

Formerly the Towe Ford Museum, in 1987 the museum showcased the largest collection of Fords in the world from the collection of Montana banker Edward Towe. Today, drawing from its own collection and loans, visitors can view cars from 1885 to recent models.

California Automobile Museum
(top and bottom)

The California Automobile Museum show-cases over 150 cars—classics, race cars, muscle cars, and early cars. It holds an inventory of available cars for purchase as well. Its mission is to preserve, exhibit, and to tell the story of the automobile and its influence on our lives.

Sacramento History Museum *(top and bottom)*

The Sacramento History Museum delves deep into the city's rich history, including the California Gold Rush, mining, fur trapping, Nisenan and Maidu Indian Nations, agriculture, and cultural heritage. Interactive exhibits help visitors understand the early events and unique people who helped shape the great state of California.

Golden 1 Center

Home to the NBA Sacramento Kings, this impressive center opened as an indoor multi-use facility in October 2016. Towering 16-stories and with a capacity of over 17,000, the amazing venue hosts concerts, trade shows, rodeos, ice shows, family events, and more.

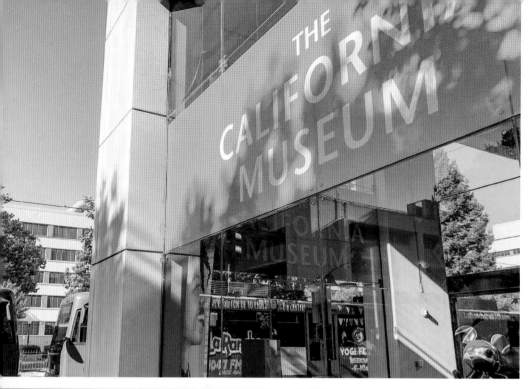

The California Museum *(top and bottom)*

Opened in 1998, the museum presents stories on the contributions of women and other groups. Located in the California State Archives building, the museum is also home to the California Hall of Fame honoring legendary individuals and families who embody the spirit of California and have made their mark on history.

Constitution Wall

Inspirational words are sculpted into this six-story wall at the entry of the California Museum. Taken from the California Constitution, words such as "rights," "assemble," and "redress" are reminders of the freedoms guaranteed to Californians. Depending on the light, different words become apparent at varying times of the day.

State Indian Museum *(above)*

Opened in 1940, the museum shares California Indian culture through three themes: nature, spirit, and family. Visitors can view an exhibit of Ishi, believed to be the last Yahi Tribe member; view cultural items such as baskets, canoes, and fishing tools—some being 2400 years old; or handle authentic tools.

Powerhouse Science Center
(opposite top and bottom)

A place for kids to participate and learn about science, this center offers changing exhibits, a planetarium, and a hands-on science lab. The center's mission is to inspire people to explore the possibilities of science with an emphasis on science, technology, engineering, and math.

Sacramento River and Tower Bridge
(top and bottom)

Day and night show a placid Sacramento River flowing below the Tower Bridge, but this belies its importance to the city and to California as a major source of commerce. Serving much of Central and Southern California, the river is used for irrigation throughout major agricultural valleys.

Crocker Art Museum *(top and bottom)*

The West's longest continuing art museum offers a large collection of California art, including Charles Christian Nahl's art of the California Gold Rush; Edward Weston's iconic photography, and the pop-art food paintings by Wayne Thiebaud. The Teel Family Pavilion opened in 2010 expanding the museum with 125,000 square feet.

Crocker Art Museum

Judge E.B. Crocker purchased this home in 1868 and had a gallery built to show-case his extensive personal art collection. Completed in 1872 and later gifted to Sacramento, the museum continued to grow in art and fame through the years. A 1989 renovation restored the mansion's exterior and created a modern gallery.

Leland Stanford Mansion *(above and right)*

Leland Stanford, Central Pacific Railroad's co-founder, purchased this home in 1861 shortly before he became governor, adding 19,000 square feet and taking the mansion up to four stories for his family's needs. His wife donated the home to the Bishop of Sacramento in 1900 as a children's home.

Memorial Auditorium (*opposite*)

With a ballroom, meeting rooms, a theater, and an exhibit hall, Memorial Auditorium has been a key venue in Sacramento since its opening in 1927. It hosts graduations, conferences, sporting events, receptions, and popular headliners including The Doobie Brothers, Josh Groban, and Melissa Etheridge.

Sacramento Convention Center (*above*)

Comprised of the Convention Center, Community Center Theater, and Historic Memorial Auditorium, the Sacramento Convention Center boasts an annual attendance of 875,000 people, 31 meeting rooms, and over 137,000 square feet of exhibit space. Twin sculptures by artist Stephen Kaltenbach grace its entrance.

Old Tavern

On the National Register of Historic Places, this building was constructed in the 1870s and served as a warehouse and distillery to Fort Sutter. It later became the Sacramento Brewery, a popular place frequented by stagecoach travelers along their journeys. Today, several businesses and a restaurant occupy its space.

CalPERS Building *(top and bottom)*

The California Public Employees Retirement System Headquarters Complex was designed by Pickard Chilton and received multiple awards including the Environmental Recognition Award in 2006. Its glass walls and trellises glisten in the Sacramento sun. An interior courtyard offers a retreat for employees and visitors.

Sacramento RT Light Rail
(above, left, and opposite)

With 70 bus routes and 43 miles of light rail, the Sacramento RT Light Rail serves about 400 square miles with 97 light rail cars, 205 buses, and 23 shuttle vans linking popular sites around town. SacRT operates 365 days a year, with light-rail trains starting at 4:00 am.

The Barn

Designed by landscape architecture firm !melk, The Barn was inspired by a sprouting vegetable seed in homage to Sacramento's huge agricultural influence. Seemingly able to defy gravity, it is the events center for the Sacramento Bridge District along the Sacramento River Walk, offering delightful, open-air venues.

Cathedral of the Blessed Sacrament
(above and opposite)

Considered a religious and civic land-mark, the cathedral, dedicated in 1889, is one of the largest west of the Mississippi River. Recently restored, the cathedral now shines with its original splendor. Located next to the Capitol and accessible by the Light Rail, it is open daily.

Bishop Gallegos *(left)*

Adjacent to the cathedral stands this life-sized statue of Alphonse Gallegos, Auxiliary Bishop of Sacramento from 1981 until his death in 1991. The bishop has been declared Venerable—one miracle away from becoming a saint. The statue was erected in 1997 in Bishop Gallegos Square.

Sacramento Historic City Cemetery
(top, bottom, and opposite)

Captain John Sutter donated 10 acres for a burial ground, marking the beginning of this Victorian-era cemetery in 1849. Many local notables are buried here including Mark Hopkins, Jr., and E.B. Crocker. Stroll the gardens, visit the plots of famous Californians, and take in the natural surroundings.

California Firefighters Memorial
(above and left)

Erected on the grounds of Capitol Park, the memorial pays tribute to all California firefighters who have died in the line of duty since 1850. The three features of the memorial include a wall etched with the firefighter names; and two bronze statues, *Fallen Brother* and *Holding the Line*.

Spanish American War Statue *(above)*

The Hiker, standing more than 8 feet tall, was erected in 1949 and placed in Capitol Park to honor California veterans from the Spanish–American War. One of more than 50 copies by sculptor Theo Alice Ruggles Kitson, it was named from the term by which soldiers referred to themselves.

USS California Bell *(right)*

Launched in 1919 at Mare Island Naval Shipyard near San Francisco, the USS *California* served as flagship for the Pacific Fleet for 20 years. Later moved to Pearl Harbor, she was sunk during the attack on the harbor in 1941. In 1949 her bell was placed in Capitol Park to commemorate her distinguished service.

California Vietnam Veterans Memorial
(top and bottom)

Dedicated in 1988 and located in Capitol Park near the rose garden, the memorial is made up of a series of granite panels engraved with the 5,673 names of Californians who were lost in the Vietnam War. In the center is a bronze statue depicting a 19-year-old combat soldier.

Veterans Memorial

A moving remembrance of the five million Californians who served their country since 1850. Dedicated in 1998 and located in Capitol Park, the obelisk is etched with images ranging from soldiers and their everyday life to their families welcoming them home. Slices through the panels symbolize the devastation of war.

Thomas Star King Memorial
(above and left)

After spending 78 years in the National Statuary Hall in Washington, D.C., the statue of Thomas Starr King is now located near the entrance to the Civil War Memorial Grove in Capitol Park. King, called "The Apostle of Liberty," was an advocate for the Union cause during the Civil War.

WWI Memorial (above)

Dedicated in 1926, this stone memorial features an impressive eagle with wings spread over its nest. The plaque reads: "Dedicated to those from Sacramento County who served their country in the World War 1914-1918 and to the memory of those who gave the last full measure of devotion."

Theodore Dehone Judah (right)

Judah was known for his fervent support and design of the First Transcontinental Railroad, a 1912-mile railroad constructed between 1863-1869. He, along with miner Daniel Strong, discovered the route for a railroad to cross the Sierra Nevadas. Judah was also responsible for securing investors for the Central Pacific Railroad.

Cesar Chavez Park *(above and right)*

Two monuments, one honoring Cesar Chavez, a renowned Latino civil rights activist, and A.J Stevens, master mechanic for the Southern Pacific Railroad and friend to labor, are both located here. *Cesar Marching to Sacramento* (above) is by artist Lisa Reinertson. The Stevens monument (right) was erected by his coworkers.

Cesar Chavez Park *(opposite)*

Developed in 1849, John Sutter, Jr. dedicated 10 "public squares" for public use. Named Cesar Chavez Park in 1999 to honor the leader of the largest farm workers union in the United States, today, the space features the Coleman Fountain and is host to summer concerts, rallies, and a famers' market.

Chinatown Mall *(top and bottom)*

This area was home to the Chinese immigrant population in Sacramento during the Gold Rush. Today, the Chinatown Mall is where people come to enjoy the culture and history as well as the arts of the Chinese-American community. The entrance to the mall is adorned with a decorative gate.

Dr. Sun Yat Sen *(opposite)*

Located in the Chinatown Mall is a statue of Dr. Sun Yat Sen, a revolutionary who aided in the uprising that ended more than 2,000 years of imperial rule in China. He became the first Provisional President of the Republic of China, establishing a government with basic laws of the land.

McKinley Park *(top and bottom)*

Custom designed and recently renovated,
the McKinley Park Playground includes
a river boat, street trolley, a large tree
house, rubber surfacing, a climbing wall,
and large boulders. A colorful tile mural
depicting lion fish was installed and
painted by local Sacramento artists.

McKinley Park

While the children enjoy the playground, adults have their own areas of the park to enjoy, including a basketball court, community center, pools, tennis courts, garden and arts center, picnic area, horseshoe pits, jogging trails, soccer and softball fields, and a volleyball court.

Frederick N. Evans Memorial Rose Garden *(above, left, and opposite)*

Named after its original designer and located within McKinley Park, the garden displays 1,200 rose bushes and is available for special events. Evans wanted the garden to be educational, "where Sacramentans interested in flowers and plants may come and study their culture."

Sutter's Fort *(opposite top and bottom)*

Constructed in 1840 by Sacramento's founder John Sutter as an agricultural and trade colony, Sutter's Fort had mostly been abandoned after the discovery of gold at Sutter's Mill. Today, this reconstructed compound portrays life in the 1840s and is open year-round.

Sacramento Bee Door *(above)*

Now hidden below an offramp off I-5 between J and K streets, this remnant is where the original *Sacramento Bee* daily newspaper building was constructed in 1857. Its first building was a two-story brick structure and its door to the past still interests visitors today.

Fabulous Forties Homes
(top and bottom, and opposite)

Nestled in the East Sacramento district, on 38th to 48th street and between J Street and Folsom Blvd., the Fab Forties neighborhood had the largest lots, allowing for larger homes to be built. The homes and gardens are spectacular and make it a highly prized area in which to live.

Fall in Sacramento *(top and bottom)*

Fall foliage, crisp temperatures, and frost on pumpkins all give Sacramentans something to get excited about, especially after a long hot summer. Football games, apple picking, city walks, the Sacramento Harvest Festival, and river cruises are great ways to spend time outdoors.

Fall in Sacramento *(top and bottom)*

An afternoon at a pumpkin farm is the perfect way to enjoy an autumn day and the spectacular colors that the season brings. There are many other events to enjoy this time of year as well, including the Autumn Equinox Celebration, the California Capital Airshow, and the Sacramento Home & Garden Show.

Deep Water Ship Channel
(opposite top and bottom)

This inland port, now called Port of West Sacramento, was opened to deep-sea traffic in 1963 and serves the Northern California rice industry. The Sacramento Deep Water Ship Channel is 30 feet deep and 43 miles long, specializing in break-bulk, agriculture, bulk, and construction cargo.

Port of Sacramento *(above)*

The Port of Sacramento is part of the California Green Trade Corridor Project to improve the movement of cargo throughout Northern California. This project reduces freight traffic on Interstate 580 by shipping along the waterways between ports of Oakland, Stockton and Sacramento, instead of along the roadways.

Sailing on Sacramento River *(top)*

What better way could there be to fully appreciate the river than being on it? Sail, or even learn to sail, in the serene, cool waters of the Sacramento River. Here, Laser sailors from a local yacht club enjoy a friendly race.

Waterskiing *(bottom)*

Live along the water, play along the water. Water skiing in the river and the delta offers outdoor recreationists an exhilarating water experience. Enjoy the river any way you like—be it sailing, fishing, or sitting along its green shores. Enjoy a family picnic at the water's edge and have fun.

I St. Bridge (above)

Built in 1911 and weighing over 7 million pounds, the I Street Bridge has two decks, one for cars and one for the railroad. Its center swings 90 degrees on a pedestal to allow boats to pass. This more than 100-year-old bridge handles roughly 80 trains per day.

Guy West Bridge (pages 102–103)

Designed to emulate the Golden Gate Bridge, this suspension bridge, for pedestrians and bicycle traffic, spans the American River in Sacramento and links California State University Sacramento with Campus Commons. It was known as the longest pedestrian suspension bridge in the country at the time it opened in 1967.

International World Peace Rose Gardens *(above, left, and opposite)*

This Victorian-style garden, with its pathways and fountain, was established in 2003 in Capitol Park and dedicated to women, children, and families. Created as a sanctuary of peace and love for all people, nations, and religions, it offers over 650 roses and more than 153 varieties.

Fairytale Town *(top and bottom)*

Located in William Land Park, this literacy-based park opened in 1959. Many renovations have been made to the park through the years. It now offers 25 nursery rhyme and fairytale playsets along with friendly farm animals, gardens, and two stages for performances. The park welcomes roughly 230,000 guests annually.

Funderland *(top, bottom, and right)*

Originally Land Park Kiddie Land, Funder-land began thrilling kids in 1946 with amusement rides. The two-acre park, located in William Land Park, has been completely renovated and landscaped. Spinning Teacups was added at that time and remains a park favorite for young children.

Sacramento Zoo *(above and right)*

Located in William Land Park, the Sacramento Zoo opened in 1927 with 40 animals. Giraffes are a favorite of the visitors and staff alike. A new heated and more spacious barn and yard were constructed for the giraffes in 2009. The space includes a breeding facility and larger stalls. The *Tall Wonders* exhibit gives visitors a chance to see these animals eye to eye.

Sacramento Zoo *(opposite top and bottom)*

Many species and interesting enclosures have been added since the zoo opened. Today, more than 500 rare and endangered animals are housed at the zoo. Popular exhibits include the colorful flamingos and the ever fascinating chimpanzees. Connect with nature through education, conservation, and appreciation.

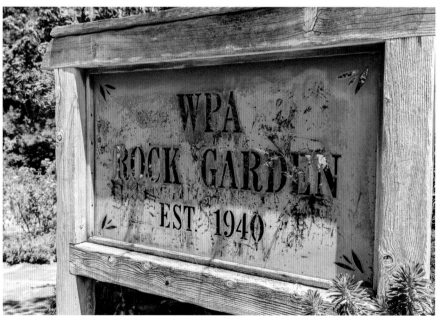

William Land Park Rock Garden
(above and left)

In 1911, William Land, a Sacramento businessman, bequest $250,000 for this park. Later, the Work Projects Administration of the 40s employed artisans and craftspeople to improve the city and the WPA Rock Garden was added. Now a major city park, it is enjoyed by families year-round.

Discovery Park *(above and right)*

Part of the American River Parkway, Discovery Park is located at the confluence of the American River and the Sacramento River. Discovery Park is not just a 302-acre recreational park, it is also part of the Sacramento flood-control system. An archery range, softball field, and fishing are a few of the recreational offerings.

Discovery Park

Wildlife abounds for the nature lover when they bike or stroll through Discovery Park along the 32-mile Jedediah Smith Bike Trail. Boaters find one of the best boat launches in the county and great fishing opportunities. There are plenty of quiet places to just sit and enjoy nature too.

Golden State Triathlon *(above and right)*

The Golden State Triathlon is California's only criterium sprint triathlon. Starting in Discovery Park, athletes swim across the river before beginning the 15-mile, 3-loop bike course and 3-mile run along the American River to complete the event. There is also a shorter, Super Sprint Triathlon. This is all followed by a fabulous party.

Making Strides Breast Cancer Walk
(above and left)

Beginning at the Capitol Building and making their way over the Tower Bridge, thousands of participants walk to help fight cancer. Each event raises money to promote awareness, fund innovative research, and celebrate survivors while helping to remember loved ones.

Amgen Tour (above and right)

The excitement is palpable at the beginning of the Amgen Tour of California. The seven-day, men-only event covers over 600 miles along city streets, highways, and the coast. The Amgen Tour of California Women's Race runs three days concurrently. Both races attract top cyclists from around the world.

California Capital Airshow
(above and left)

The nonprofit California Capital Airshow has been offering thrills since 2004. This popular event features some of the best military and civilian aviators in the world, including the daredevils of the United States Air Force Thunderbirds.

California Capital Airshow
(above and right)

Through displays of historic aircraft and high-flying stunts, the California Capital Airshow honors the region's aviation heritage, inspiring those who dare to dream of someday harnessing the exhilarating power of flight.

California State Fair
(top, bottom, and opposite)

Neon lights, a Ferris wheel, and the ultimate flying swing attract people from across the state. Running for 17 days, the fair draws attendance of over 570,000 people. Dedicated to California's achievements, agriculture, traditions and diversity of people since 1854.

4th of July Fireworks
(top, bottom, and opposite)

A full day of events around Sacramento culminate in a spectacular fireworks extravaganza. The Fourth on the Field at Raley's Field is a prime location for viewing fireworks. But the spectacular show above the Sacramento skyline and Tower Bridge is magical from any location.

California State University (top and bottom)

First known as Sacramento State College in 1947, California State University is informally called "Sac State." Nestled along the American River on 300 acres, typical enrollment is just over 28,000 students per year with 151 Bachelor's degrees, 69 Master's degrees, 28 teaching credentials, and 2 Doctoral degrees.

Tree Campus USA (opposite top and bottom)

With more than 3,500 trees, Sac State has been honored as a Tree Campus USA. Many of the campus' trees date back to 1953 when saplings were planted helping to establish the abundance of trees that now shade the campus. There are more than 20 species of oak and pine throughout the campus.

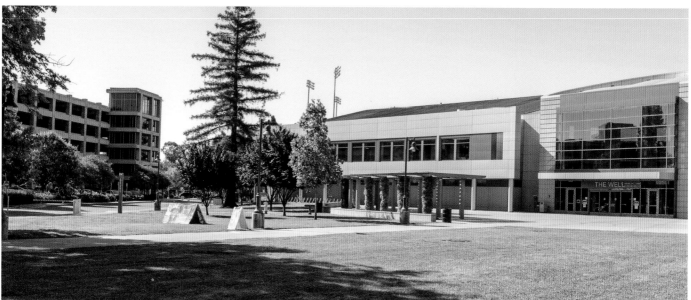

California State University *(top and bottom)*

The varied steel and glass architecture contrast the natural surroundings of this city campus. In 2010 an initiative was launched focusing on a more welcoming campus culture and environment, and several new buildings were constructed including a residence hall, research center, and bookstore.

California State University
(opposite top and bottom)

Biking between buildings is a healthy and fun way to get to class. Three free bicycle compounds are located on campus to help promote cycling. While cycling on campus, look for *Soft-Hearted*, located near Sequoia Hall, by artist, Gerald Walburg.

Raley Field (above, left, and opposite)

Home of the Sacramento River Cats, a Triple-A, minor-league baseball team affiliated with the San Francisco Giants, Raley Field was built in 2007 on the site of old warehouses and railyards. Today, with a capacity of over 14,000, Raley Field hosts games, concerts, and provides a number of excellent venues for private events.

Steve Pate-Newberry calls Sacramento, California, his home. With his high school sweetheart (now wife) and two grown children, Steve strives to capture moments—to transport his viewers to smell the sun-kissed fields of lavender, feel the spray of the cascading waterfalls at Yosemite, and marvel at the Milky Way galaxy in the night's sky. His professional career has taken him to some of the world's most beautiful landscapes in Greece, Italy, France, England, Mexico, and Canada. Many of his works can be seen in commercial offices throughout Northern California. In addition to landscapes, Steve is one of the premiere events and convention photographers in Northern California. He has worked with some of the top associations and corporations such as Meeting Planners International, the California Society of Association Executives, The NFL Pro Football Hall of Fame, Centene Corporation, Colgate, and many others. To learn more about Steve's work please visit www.spnphotography.com.

Michelle Alberigi McKenzie is a writer and editor. Her clients have included the Monterey Bay Aquarium, *California Retired Teachers Association Magazine, CONTACT*, as well as authors, coaches, and wellness professionals. She's a published author of three children's books and a recipient of the Children's Choice List 2002 Award–Children's Literature. A former publisher for the Monterey Bay Aquarium, she has worked on many natural history books for adults and children. Today, Michelle is also an antiques dealer, a certified life coach, and writes animal welfare grants for nonprofits. A California native, Michelle is based out of Grass Valley, California, where she lives with her husband, dogs, cats, horse, and donkey. To learn more about Michelle please visit McKenziebookworks.com.